ADOPTION IS FOR ALWAYS

Linda Walvoord Girard

Illustrations by Judith Friedman

ALBERT WHITMAN & COMPANY, NILES, ILLINOIS

With thanks to Nancy Claassen, M.F.W. and adoptive parent;
Pat Dreibelbis, M.F.W.;
Brian Fassler, my nephew;
Karen Lundgren, R.N., adoptee, birthmother, and adoptive parent;
Thelma Stevens, preschool teacher;
Margaret Svetlauskas, M.F.W., A.C.S.W.;
Marilyn Witt, adoptive parent.

Library of Congress Cataloging-in-Publication Data

Girard, Linda Walvoord.
   Adoption is for always.

   *Summary: Although Celia reacts to having been
adopted with anger and insecurity, her parents help
her accept her feelings and celebrate their love for
her by making her adoption day a family holiday.
Includes factual information about the adoption
process.*
   *[1. Adoption—Fiction] I. Friedman, Judith,
1945-   ill. II. Title.*
PZ7.G43953Ad 1986   [Fic]   86-15843
ISBN 0-8075-0185-9 (lib. bdg.)

The text of the book is printed in fourteen-point Garth Graphic.

*Text © 1986 by Linda Walvoord Girard
Illustrations © 1986 by Judith Friedman
Published in 1986 by Albert Whitman & Company, Niles, Illinois
Published simultaneously in Canada by General Publishing, Limited, Toronto
Printed in U.S.A. All rights reserved.
10   9   8   7   6   5   4   3   2   1*

To all adopted children and their parents. L.W.G.
To Julie, with thanks. J.F.

Ever since Celia was a tiny girl, her mother and father had told her she was adopted. They said she hadn't grown inside her mommy but had grown inside a lady called her birthmother.

Celia hadn't really heard what they said. When her parents said, "Celia, we adopted you," it sounded no different than, "Celia, we took you to the park when you were a baby."

One Saturday, Celia and her parents were sitting on the porch swing. Mother said, "We bought this swing right after we adopted you." That day, Celia really heard the words. *Adopted*! This time she understood. Just like the baby down the street, Celia was adopted!

"You mean that birthmother lady was my mommy first, before you? And somebody else was my daddy?"

Mother nodded, yes.

"You mean I have another mommy somewhere?"

Daddy nodded. "She was your mommy just in the very beginning," he said.

Celia felt her stomach hurt. "But I don't want to be adopted!" she said. "I want you and Mommy to be my ONLY mommy and daddy!"

Celia went to her room and lay on the bed. She felt confused, as if someone had played a trick on her. A birthmother was a *mommy*! She buried her head in the pillow.

Celia stayed in her room and watched her goldfish for a long time. Being adopted made her feel alone.

Then her parents came to the door.

"We know you feel sad, Celia," Mother said. "But we are your mommy and daddy now. We've belonged to each other since you were four days old. Look, we've got your baby book!"

Her mother showed Celia pictures she'd seen before, from the time she was a tiny baby.

"Here's you drooling, and here's you in the bathtub, and here's you in front of a mirror, and here's you in your baby buggy, and here's you with Grandpa, and here's you playing in the mud!" her mother said. She and Daddy were laughing, and Celia began to laugh, too. There were so many photos of Celia they were falling out of the pages.

Celia felt a little better then. Nobody said anything more about adoption that night, but when Daddy tucked her in, he said, "You're ours for keeps, Pumpkin," and he hugged her extra tight.

Still, Celia lay awake a long time that night. She couldn't forget that word, *adopted*. Ugh. It couldn't be a word about her. She tried to pretend it wasn't true, but lying in bed, she started thinking. If she wasn't born out of Mother's body, then whose baby was she? She wondered who her birthparents were, and why they didn't keep her. Had she been a bad baby, or an ugly one?

Celia woke up feeling grumpy and sad. That morning she got into trouble. She didn't pick up her clothes after Mother asked twice. She had to stay in her room.

"I don't like you!" she yelled when she came back down. "You're not beautiful like my real mommy! She was a movie star! And my daddy was a football player!" Celia just made that up to make her mother feel bad.

"I know you're angry, but that doesn't mean you can say hurtful things," Mother said quietly. "You have to mind my rules, and that's that. I AM your real mommy now."

The next week, Celia's mother brought home a library book about a baby being adopted, but Celia didn't read it.

"It's not about me! Take it back!" she said.

Her mother didn't, so Celia threw the book under the sofa. She wished her parents hadn't ever told her she was adopted.

The next time Nancy, the sitter, came, Celia asked her to read the library book. She wanted to know if adopted children can ever be sent back to their birthmothers. What if a lady knocked on the door one day and said, "Hi, I'm your mommy. It's time for you to come home, Stephanie"? What if you didn't even know your name was Stephanie?

Celia sat on Nancy's lap and listened. The book said no one can change an adoption. When a judge says you're adopted, you're not borrowed, and you're not just visiting. The book said adoption is for always.

At bedtime, Celia put the book under her pillow.

One day Celia and her mother were folding clothes. Mother smelled good because she'd just put on some perfume called Josephine. She let Celia put some on, too. Celia asked, "Was Josephine my birthmother's name?"

"Your birthmother's name was Susan," Mother said. "We never met her, but she wrote us a letter. She was very sad when she had to let you go."

That's all Celia wanted to hear right then. She went and turned on the TV.

Everything went round and round in her head. She watched three programs and never heard a single word. Her birthmother was sad to let her go. Adoption is forever, and she could never lose the mother and father she had now. Her birthmother's name was Susan. *SusanSusanSusan.*

On Valentine's Day, Celia drew a heart that said *Susan.*

"What's my father's name?" Celia asked Daddy one night.

"Walter," Daddy said, pointing to himself. "That's me!"

Celia laughed. Then Daddy gave her a squeeze. "You mean your birthfather, I know!"

"We don't know his name," Mother said. "But of course you do have a birthfather, and Susan knew who he was."

"But where did they live?"

"That's just it," Daddy said. "They didn't live in the same place, and they weren't married. So they didn't have a home to give you."

"It's the sad part of your story," Mother said.

"But it was happy for us," Daddy added. "Remember that."

"Where was I born?"

"In a hospital near here," Daddy said.

Celia didn't know if she wanted to ask more. She went outside to play on the swing.

Celia thought about her birthparents when she was in the bathtub. She thought about them in church while everyone sang songs. She thought about them when she was in school.

"Do all mothers love their children?" Celia asked her teacher, Mrs. Thomas.

"I think your birthmother loved you," Mrs. Thomas said. She seemed to know just what Celia was thinking.

"How do you know?" Celia asked.

"She had to love you in order to give you up," her teacher said.

Mrs. Thomas got a picture out of her purse. "This is my baby," she said. "I know how hard it must be for a mommy to say goodbye forever to a new baby. Even if she couldn't keep you, she still wanted you to be loved and taken care of. Your birthmother did that for you."

Celia had known Mrs. Thomas a long time. Mrs. Thomas hugged the children as they came in, and she helped them with their boots all winter without ever getting cross. She talked to all the parents, too. Mrs. Thomas knew lots about mothers and children.

Celia skipped all the way home. "Guess what!" she said at supper. "Mrs. Thomas says when you're adopted, it means your birthparents took care of you the best way they could. They loved you."

"Of course they did!" Daddy said.

"Then there was nothing wrong with me?" Celia asked.

"There was *nothing* wrong with you," Daddy said. "And you didn't do anything wrong. Babies who get adopted have never done anything wrong."

"Where was I when you met me?" Celia asked.

"At the hospital," Mother said. "You were four days old. A lady from the adoption agency met us there."

"When we saw you, it was love at first sight," Daddy said.

"Then was I all adopted?" Celia asked.

"Not quite," said Mother. "Adoptions are made final by a judge. Your birthmother filled out papers. We filled out papers. Her papers said she was not able to be your mommy anymore. Our papers said we would be good parents and wanted you. So one winter day, we went to the courthouse with you all bundled up. There was the judge in his robe. Daddy and I stood before him, and he looked at all the papers. He said, 'Do you promise to love this baby for always, and be her parents, no matter what, rain or shine?'

"'We do!' we said.

"'Will you take care of her and teach her until she's all grown up?'

"'We will!' we said.

"'Very good,' said the judge, and he signed the papers that day."

"Then you could never let me go?" Celia asked.

"Never, never," said Mother.

"You'll always be our girl, no matter what, even if you grow green spots," Daddy said.

"If you have a baby someday, we'll be the grandparents," Mother said.

"We went from the courtroom to a party," said Daddy.

"A party for me?"

"Of course. Just the three of us, and about a million friends and relatives," Mother said. "With cake and ice cream and balloons. A welcome party for the baby we had waited for so long."

Daddy picked Celia up.

"We're glad your birthparents gave you life, and glad the agency helped us find you, and glad the judge signed the papers. Now we're a family. But every year on your adoption day, Mommy and I remember the special way you came to us. Lots of children in the world are adopted, but there's only one Celia O'Shaunessy.

"Now, I have a terrific idea. Every year, on that day, shall we have another party, just us three?"

Celia hugged Daddy so tightly his jacket buttons made marks in her cheek. It felt all right now. It was okay that she wasn't born to her mommy and daddy, like most kids are. It was okay about Susan and her other father, too. She had a birthday and an adoption day. From now on they'd celebrate both of them. There'd be lots of cake, and balloons.